I0011387

DOCKER in Use

Exploration of Docker in Details

By Harry Colvin

Copyright©2015 Harry Colvin
All Rights Reserved

Copyright © 2015 by Harry Colvin.

All rights reserved. No part of this publication may be reproduced, distributed, or transmitted in any form or by any means, including photocopying, recording, or other electronic or mechanical methods, without the prior written permission of the author, except in the case of brief quotations embodied in critical reviews and certain other noncommercial uses permitted by copyright law.

Table of Contents

Disclaimer

While all attempts have been made to verify the information provided in this book, the author does assume any responsibility for errors, omissions, or contrary interpretations of the subject matter contained within. **The information provided in this book is for educational and entertainment purposes only. The reader is responsible for his or her own actions and the author does not accept any responsibilities for any liabilities or damages, real or perceived, resulting from the use of this information.**

The trademarks that are used are without any consent, and the publication of the trademark is without permission or backing by the trademark owner. All trademarks and brands within this book are for clarifying purposes only and are the owned by the owners themselves, not affiliated with this document.

Introduction

The Docker is a tool which is highly used in production environments. This is why you need to know how to perform complex tasks with the Docker. The Docker command line is very powerful. You need to understand how to use most of the commands for it.

This will make you a Docker expert. The security of the Docker should be highly enhanced. This will help in the safeguarding of the data and information which is sensitive. There are measures which can be taken to prevent this, and these will be discussed in this book. Networking for the Docker is also crucial. Learn how to work with the Docker ports, and how to enhance communication between Docker containers.

Chapter 1- How to work with Docker images, command line tools, and containers

Installation of the Docker is a very simple process. If you don't know how to do it consult with the book "Docker. The first look" by Kevin Watts.

Building a Docker image

One can choose to build their own Docker image, and then use it on their system. The image can also be uploaded to the Docker Registry, such as the Docker Hub. If uploaded on the private registry, you will be able to down access it. If you load and then use it on your system, others will not be able to access it. If you upload it to a public registry, the others will be able to access the image, download it, and then use it on their systems. This means that you will have shared your Docker image.

In this section, we will guide you on how to improve the whalesay image by building a new version of it. Follow the steps given below:

1. Writing to the Dockerfile

This will be written in a text file. This file will be used to describe the software which will be used to make the image. It will also be responsible for specifying the environment and the commands to be used. Just open your terminal. You can then find the boot2docker icon and then click on it.

2. Clicking on it will open the boot2docker terminal. Move your cursor to the prompt of this terminal.

3. We then need to create a new directory. This can be done by use of the following command:

```
$ mkdir dockerdirectory
```

The directory will provide us with a context for building the image, meaning that it will act as a store for the components necessary for building of the image.

4. You can then change to the directory which we have built above. This can be done by use of the following command:

$ cd dockerdirectory

Note that the directory has nothing at the moment. We need to create a Dockerfile in the directory. This can be done by use of the following command:

$ touch Dockerfile

After typing the above command, just hit the *"Return"* key. The command will create the file in the directory. To verify whether this succeeded, type the following command:

```
$ ls Dockerfile
Dockerfile
```

This shows that the file was successfully created.

5. We now need to open the file which we have created so that we can add something to it. Just run the following command:

```
$ open -e Dockerfile
```

Once you have typed the above command, just hit the *"Return"* key. The text editor will be opened as follows:

Note that the file has nothing in it at the moment.

6. In the file, add the following command:

```
FROM docker/whalesay:latest
```

The keyword *"FROM"* has been used so as to tell the Docker the kind of image which it will be based on, which in this case is the *"whalesay"* image. The next step is the addition of the program *"fortune"* to the image.

7. Add the following line of command to the file:

```
RUN apt-get -y update && apt-get install -y fortunes
```

With the above command, our whalesay image will be able to print out some messages. These will be picked randomly. We have used the program *"apt-get"* so as to install the fortunes in our computer. If you have added the words correctly, then it will work effectively, so you do not have to worry about what they mean too much.

8. We now need to instruct the software to execute the image after the process of loading it is complete. However, this should be done once the image has been obtained completely. Just add the following command to the file:

CMD /usr/softwares/fortunes -a | cowsay

With the above line, the fortunes program will be able to send its quotes the above program, which is *"cowsay."*

9. You can then save your file together with its changes. Just click on *"File"* and then choose *"Save."* After that, you will be ready to build your image since all of the ingredients or the requirements are ready.

Building the image

We now need to build the image from the Dockerfile which we have just created. To do this, just follow the steps given below:

1. Open the boot2docker terminal, and then place your cursor at its prompt.

2. Type the following command in the terminal:

```
cat Dockerfile
```

   This should tell you whether or not the file is in the current directory.

3. On the same terminal, type the following command:

```
docker build -t docker-whale .
```

   Once you type the command, just press the _"Return"_ key and observe what happens. You will see the following from the command:

```
Sending build context to Docker daemon 158.8 M
...snip...
Removing intermediate container a8e6faa88df3
Successfully built 7d9495d03763
```

This shows that the command will run in a verbose manner. The command will take some time to run, so just wait for it to complete. Take care not to forget the period (.) at the end of the command as this will result into errors. The image will then be ready for use. However, before starting to use it, you need to understand the build process of the Dockerfile. This is discussed in the next section.

The build process

The command `docker build -t docker-whale .` is responsible for the build process of the image. What it did is that it takes the image which is located in the current directory. An image is built from this image, and it is named *"docker-whale."* It is then stored in the local machine. You noticed that the command took more than a minute to run, and the output from it is long and looks complex.

The first thing that the docker does is to check whether all the materials which are needed for the image to be built are available. The following command is responsible for this:

```
Sending build context to Docker daemon 158.8 MB
```

The Docker will then be loaded with the whalesay image. For most of you, this image is locally available, that is, in your local machine. This means that there is no need for the Docker to download this image. This is done in the following step:

```
Step 0 : FROM docker/whalesay:latest
 ---> fb434121fc77
```

The next step of the Docker involves the updating of the package manager. In this case, it uses the *"apt-get"* command so as to accomplish this task.

```
RUN apt-get -y update && apt-get install -y fortunes
```

It will run verbosely, so you don't have to understand each of the lines which it outputs.

```
---> Running in 27d224dfa5b2
Ign http://archive.ubuntu.com trusty InRelease
Ign http://archive.ubuntu.com trusty-updates InRelease
Ign http://archive.ubuntu.com trusty-security InRelease
Hit http://archive.ubuntu.com trusty Release.gpg
....snip...
Get:15 http://archive.ubuntu.com trusty-security/restricted amd64 Packages [14.8 kB]
Get:16 http://archive.ubuntu.com trusty-security/universe amd64 Packages [134 kB]
Reading package lists...
```

The new *"fortunes"* software will then be installed by the Docker. The following command will be used for this purpose:

```
RUN apt-get install -y fortunes
```

Again, the command will run verbosely, meaning that you will be informed of how it is progressing. You will observe output similar to the one shown in the figure given below:

```
---> Running in 23aa52c1897c
Reading package lists...
Building dependency tree...
Reading state information...
The following extra packages will be installed:
  fortune-mod fortunes-min librecode0
Suggested packages:
  x11-utils bsdmainutils
The following NEW packages will be installed:
  fortune-mod fortunes fortunes-min librecode0
0 upgraded, 4 newly installed, 0 to remove and 3 not upgrade
Need to get 1961 kB of archives.
```

The build process will then be completed, and the Docker will show what it has achieved.

```
---> Running in a8e6faa88df3
---> 7d9495d03763
Removing intermediate container a8e6faa88df3
Successfully built 7d9495d03763
```

Running the new Docker-whale image

Now that you have built a new image, you need to verify and then run it. To do this, follow the steps given below:

1. Open the boot2docker terminal, and then place your cursor at its prompt.

2. Type the command *"docker images"* and then press the *"Return"* key.

   The command will list all of the images which are available in your local machines. The new image, that is, the *"Docker-whale"* should be in the list. This is shown in the figure given below:

   ```
   $ docker images
   REPOSITORY          TAG
   docker-whale        latest
   ```

3. We then need to run the new image. On the same terminal, just type the command "docker run docker-whale" and then hit the *"Return"* key.

```
$ docker run docker-whale
```

If the configuration was well done, you will notice that the Docker image is capable of displaying its own messages when being launched. These messages are picked at random. The command line will also somehow be smaller compared to the previous image. If you are good at observing, you will also realize that the Docker downloaded nothing, since everything was available in the local machine. You are now aware of how you can create your own image.

The Docker command line

In case the Docker daemon you are using is a remote one, such as the boot2docker, then avoid using the *"sudo"* command before your commands.

If you need to know the commands which are supported by the Docker, just open the terminal and then run the command *"docker"* or *"docker help."* This is shown below:

```
$ docker
  Usage: docker [OPTIONS] COMMAND [arg...]
    -H, --host=[]: The socket(s) to bind to in daemon mode, specified using one or more †

  A self-sufficient runtime for Linux containers.
```

If you have to use the *"sudo"* command before the docker commands, then avoid this by creating a group named *"docker"* and then add users to it.

If you need some help on the use of any of the Docker commands, just type the command and then follow it with the *"—help"* option. An example of this is given below:

```
$ docker run --help

Usage: docker run [OPTIONS] IMAGE [COMMAND] [ARG...]

Run a command in a new container

  -a, --attach=[]              Attach to STDIN, STDOUT or STDERR
  -c, --cpu-shares=0           CPU shares (relative weight)
```

The *"attach"* command

The command takes the following syntax:

```
docker attach [OPTIONS] CONTAINER
```

With this command, one can attach to a container which is already running by use of its ID or name, so that one can control how it works in an interactive manner or just to observe its output. The same contained process can be contained several times or view the process which has been demonized very quickly.

It is also possible for us to detach from a certain container, and then leave it running. This can be done by pressing the key "*CTRL –p*" or "*CTRL –q*" which will lead to a quiet exit or by pressing "*CTRL –c*" in case the value of "*—sig—proxy*" is false. In case the value of this property is true, then the "*CTRL –c*" will lead to sending of a "*SIGINT*" to the container.

Note that if a process is running inside a Linux container and it has a PID of 1, then it will be treated specially.

However, it is recommended that the input to the Docker "*attach*" command should not be redirected.
Consider the example given below:

```
$ docker run --name test -d -it debian

275c42472aebd87c926d4527885cc09f2f6db21d978c75f0a1c211c03d4bcfab

$ docker attach test

$$ exit 13

exit

$ echo $?

13

$ docker ps -a | grep test

275c44472aeb debian:7 "/bin/bash" 30 seconds ago Exited (13) 19 seconds ago

test
```

The "build" command

With this command, a Docker image is built from the Dockerfile and it will be having a context. The context of the build is the files which are located in the specified URL or Path. The command takes the following syntax:

```
docker build [OPTIONS] PATH | URL | -
```

Any files which are in the context can be referred by the build context. An example of this is an *"ADD"* instruction which can refer to any of the files in the directory.

In case you need to use a directory named *"docker"* in a branch named *"container,"* then use the command given below:

```
$ docker build https://github.com/docker/rootfs.git#container:docker
```

Other than specifying the context, a single Dockerfile can be passed in the URL. The file can also be piped via *"STDIN."* + This can be done as shown below:

```
docker build - < Dockerfile
```

If the URL or the STDIN are used, the contents will be placed in a file named *"Dockerfile"* by the system. If you have used the option *"-f"* or *"-f,"* this will be ignored. The purpose of the command *"docker build"* is responsible for looking for the Dockerfile in the build context. When you use the option *"-f"* or *"-file,"* an alternative file will be specified which can be used instead.

In case the connection to the daemon is lost, the build process will be terminated. This can happen in a case of interruption of the Docker client or in case it is killed.

Return code

If the Docker *"build"* command runs successfully, then it should return 0. In case the command fails, then a result other than 0 will be returned. If this is the case, then the reason or the cause of the failure should be part of the output. An example is shown in the figure given below:

```
$ docker build -t fail .

Sending build context to Docker daemon 2.148 kB

Sending build context to Docker daemon

Step 0 : FROM busybox

---> 59876cf8d1634

Step 1 : RUN exit 14

---> Running in f27671ec8b0a

INFO[0000] The command [/bin/sh -c exit 13] returned a non-zero code: 14

$ echo $?

1
```

Consider the example given below:

```
$ docker build -t vieux/apache:2.0 .
```

The above command will build normally, but the resulting image will be tagged. The name of the repository will be "*vieux/apache,*" while the tag number will be 0. Consider the command given below:

```
$ docker build - < Dockerfile
```

With the above command, a file will be read from STDIN, and there will be no context. Since there is no directory, there will be no sending of the contents of any local directory to our Docker daemon. The *"ADD"* for Docker will only work to a remote URL since there is no context.

Consider the command given below:

```
$ docker build - < context.tar.gz
```

With the above command, an image will be created, but the context will be the compressed read which is read from STDIN. Consider the next command given below:

```
$ docker build github.com/creack/docker-firefox
```

With the above command, the GitHub repository will be cloned, and this repository will then be used as the context. The Dockerfile located at the root of this repository will then be used as our Dockerfile. In case you need to specify an arbitrary Git repository, use the schema *"git:// or git@."* Consider the next command given below:

```
$ docker build -f Dockerfile.debug .
```

With the above command, a file named *"Dockerfile.debug"* will be used to specify the build instructions rather than using the Dockerfile. Consider the commands given below:

```
$ docker build -f dockerfiles/Dockerfile.debug -t myapp_debug .

$ docker build -f dockerfiles/Dockerfile.prod -t myapp_prod .
```

With the above commands, the current build context will be built, and this will be done in the way specified by the ".". Note that this will be done twice. If a debug version of the Dockerfile is the one you are using, then this will be done once, whereas if you are using a production version of the same, then it will also be done once. Consider the commands given below:

```
$ cd /home/usr/app/sm/dir/actually/deep

$ docker build -f /home/usr/app/dockerfiles/debug /home/usr/app

$ docker build -f ../../../../dockerfiles/debug /home/usr/app
```

The above commands will just do the same thing. Rather than using the Dockerfile, they will use the *"debug"* file and the root of the build context will be the *"/home/usr/app."* You might not know where the file *"debug"* is located. This can be found in the directory structure of our build context, and this is not determined by how you refer to it on your command line.

Commit

This command is used when we need to save the changes made to the container or its settings into a new image. With this, it will be able for you to debug the container interactively, or be able to perform an exportation of a working database to just another server. The command takes the following syntax:

```
docker commit [OPTIONS] CONTAINER [REPOSITORY[:TAG]]
```

It is highly recommended that you use Dockerfile for the management of your images in a very easy and maintainable way. Data which is saved in volumes which have been mounted in containers will not be included in the commit operation. During the commit operation, the container itself and its processes will be paused until the operation completes. This helps in avoidance of any corruption to the data which could have happened. If you use the "*—change*" option, the instructions which are contained in the Dockerfile will be applied to the image which you are creating.

Suppose that you need to commit a container, the following steps need to be followed:

Start by identifying the image and its ID. Use the following command for this purpose:

```
$ docker ps
```

Once you have identified the ID of the image, use the following command so as to commit it:

```
$ docker commit c4g779c17f0a ourimage/testimage:version3
```

You can see the ID for our image in the above command. Once you run the command *"docker images,"* you will see the new committed image being listed, which is an indication that the process ran successfully.

Once you have added new configurations to your container, you might need to save these configurations. This can be done by following the steps given below:

Begin by knowing the ID and the name of the image. This can be done by executing the following command:

```
$ docker ps
```

The image will be among the list of images displayed from the above command.
The following sequence of commands can then follow that:

```
$ docker inspect -f "{{ .Config.Env }}" c4g289e27f0b

[HOME=/ PATH=/usr/local/sbin:/usr/local/bin:/usr/sbin:/usr/bin:/sbin:/bin]

$ docker commit --change "ENV DEBUG true" c4g289e27f0b Ourimage/testimage:version3

g8283538691d

$ docker inspect -f "{{ .Config.Env }}" g8283538691d

[HOME=/ PATH=/usr/local/sbin:/usr/local/bin:/usr/sbin:/usr/bin:/sbin:/bin DEBUG=true]
```

With the above commands, the process will be done successfully.

The "create" command

This command is used for creation of a new container. The command takes the following syntax:

```
docker create [OPTIONS] IMAGE [COMMAND] [ARG...]
```

When you run the command *"docker create"* on your system, a writable container layer will be written over the image which you have specified, and it will be prepared for running of the command which you have specified. The ID of the container will be printed to the STDOUT. The difference between this command and the command *"docker –d run"* is that with this, the image will not be started. If you need to start the container at any time or point, just run the command *"docker start <container_id>."*This will let you keep the configuration of the container in such a way that it can be started at any time when needed. Examples of these are given below:

```
$ docker create -v /data --name data ubuntu
```

Just run the above command. In my case, I get the following output from it:

340633gfbb78126da76473f3d9028f6144b99c344b3261448ab190b7d961ae56

With the command, I have just created an Ubuntu image with the ID shown above. Another example is given below:

```
$ docker run --rm --volumes-from data ubuntu ls -la /data
total 8
drwxr-xr-x  2 root root 4096 Dec  5 04:10 .
drwxr-xr-x 48 root root 4096 Dec  5 04:11 ..
```

We can also use the *"create"* command for creation of a host directory bind mounted to a volume container, and we can use this in a subsequent container. This is demonstrated by the use of the commands given below:

```
$ docker create -v /home/docker:/docker --name docker ubuntu
```

The above command gives me the following output on my system:

340633gfbb78126da76473f3d9028f6144b99c344b3261448ab190b7d961ae56

This should then be followed by the following command:

```
$ docker run --rm --volumes-from docker ubuntu ls -la /docker
```

The above command gives the following output on my system:

```
total 20
drwxr-sr-x  5 1000 staff  180 Dec  5 04:00 .
drwxr-xr-x 48 root root   4096 Dec  5 04:13 ..
-rw-rw-r--  1 1000 staff 3833 Dec  5 04:01 .ash_history
-rw-r--r--  1 1000 staff  446 Nov 28 11:51 .ashrc
-rw-r--r--  1 1000 staff   25 Dec  5 04:00 .gitconfig
drwxr-sr-x  3 1000 staff   60 Dec  1 03:28 .local
-rw-r--r--  1 1000 staff  920 Nov 28 11:51 .profile
drwx--S---  2 1000 staff  460 Dec  5 00:51 .ssh
drwxr-xr-x 32 1000 staff 1140 Dec  5 04:01 docker
```

The "diff" command

This command is used to list the files and directories which have changed, and they belong to the file system of a container. The command takes the following syntax:

```
docker diff CONTAINER
```

The command also has three different events which are listed when it is executed:

- A - Add

- D - Delete

- C – Change

Consider the example given below:

```
$ docker diff 8bb0a158abfe
```

When the command is executed, the following output is observed:

```
C /dev
A /dev/kmsg
C /etc
A /etc/mtab
A /go
A /go/src
A /go/src/github.com
A /go/src/github.com/docker
A /go/src/github.com/docker/docker
A /go/src/github.com/docker/docker/.git
```

Events

The command takes the following syntax:

```
docker events [OPTIONS]
```

The Docker containers will then report the following information:

start, destroy, die, create, export, kill, , pause, oom, restart, stop, unpause

The Docker images will report the following information:

untag, delete

The parameters "*—until*" and "*—since*" can be used as UNIX timestamps which are computed relative to the time of the client machine.

If you need to listen to events as they happen in the Docker, then execute the following command:

```
$ docker events
```

For you to start and the stop the containers use the following commands:

```
$ docker start 8bb0a158abfe
```

The above command will start the container with the specified ID. To stop it from running, just use the command given below:

```
$ docker stop 8bb0a158abfe
```

At this time, you should be able to see the events since you are listening to them. If you need to show the events which have happened since a particular time, and then execute a command similar to the one given below:

```
$ docker events --since 1478316759
```

The above command will show the events which have taken place since the specified period of time. We have the time in the form of seconds. The following is a sample of the output from the above command in my system:

```
2015-02-10T17:42:14.999999999Z07:00 8bb0a158abfe: (from ubuntu-1:14.04) die
2015-05-20T17:42:14.999999999Z07:00 8bb0a158abfe: (from ubuntu-1:14.04) stop
2015-05-20T17:42:14.999999999Z07:00 7805c1d35632: (from redis:2.8) die
2015-04-20T17:42:14.999999999Z07:00 7805c1d35632: (from redis:2.8) stop
```

The command has given us the events which have taken place since the time which we have specified.

You might need to know the events which have taken place since a particular date:

```
$ docker events --since '2014-09-03'
```

The command will list all of the events which have taken place since September 3, 2014. The output might be long, depending on the time that you specify.

You might need to be very specific with respect to time. In this case, you might need to specify both the date and the exact time, in terms of hours and minutes. This can be done by use of a command similar to the one given below:

```
$ docker events --since '2014-09-03T15:38:29'
```

Just run the above command, and observe the output that you get. You might also need to get the list of events which has been generated in the previous number of minutes. This can be done by the use of a command similar to the one given below:

```
$ docker events --since '4m'
```

The above command will print all the events which have been generated in the last four minutes with respect to the current time of the system on which the command has been run on.

Filtering of events

In this case, we work with events by selecting a single or a sample of them from the available ones. Consider the command given below:

```
$ docker events --filter 'event=stop'
```

The above command will look for the running events, and then stop or terminate them. Suppose that you want to filter the Ubuntu image which is available in your system, the following command can be used for this purpose:

```
$ docker events --filter 'image=ubuntu-1:14.04'
```

You might also need to perform your filtering on the containers. A command which can be used to filter a container is given below:

```
$ docker events --filter 'container=8705c1f35643'
```

To filter more than containers at once or simultaneously, the command can be written as follows:

```
$ docker events --filter 'container=8705c1f35643'--filter 'container=8bb0a158abfe'
```

In the above command, we have specified the IDs of the two images which are to be filtered.

Consider the following command:

```
$ docker events --filter 'container=8bb0a158abfe' --filter 'event=stop'
```

What we have done is that we have filtered our container by use of its ID, and then we have terminated or stopped its process of execution. In the previous commands, we just got all of the events about the particular container whose ID we specify. In this case, we have been more specific by specifying what we want to happen.

The "exec" command

This command is used for the purpose of running a new command in a running container. It takes the following syntax:

```
docker exec [OPTIONS] CONTAINER COMMAND [ARG...]
```

This command can only run if the primary process of the container is running. This means that the PID of this process should be 1. If the container is restarted, you need not restart this command. This shows how easy it is to use. In case you pause the container while this command is executing or running, then it will fail ,and it will output an error. Let us demonstrate this by use of an example.

Suppose that we are running a container named "*mycontainer*" and at the same time this command is in execution. The execution of the container can be paused as follows:

```
$ docker pause mycontainer
```

If you run the command *"docker ps,"* you will notice that the execution has been paused. This is shown in the figure given below:

```
STATUS
Up 16 seconds (Paused)
```

You will notice the following error from the *"exec"* command which we said is in the process of execution by the time we run this command:

```
$ docker exec mycontainer ls
FATA[0000] Error response from daemon: Container mycontainer is paused, unpause the container before exec
$ echo $?
1
```

As shown in the output, it is very clear that the execution of the container has been terminated, which has caused the *"exec"* command to fail.

Consider the command given below:

```
$ docker run --name ubuntu_bash --rm -i -t ubuntu bash
```

What the command does is that it will create a new container with the name *"Ubuntu-bash."* The session for the bash will also be started once the container has been started.

Consider the command given below:

```
$ docker exec -d ubuntu_bash touch /tmp/mytasks
```

With the above command, a file named *"mytasks"* will be created in the *"/tmp"* directory inside the currently running directory, which in this case is the *"Ubuntu_bash."* Notice the use of the option *"-d."* This causes the process to be carried out in the background.

Consider the following command:

```
$ docker exec -it ubuntu_bash bash
```

With the above command, a new session of the Bash will be created in our container which is the *"Ubuntu_bash."*

The "export" command

The command is used for exportation of the contents of a particular file system into a tar archive. By default, this is then streamed to the STDOUT. The command takes the following syntax:

```
docker export [OPTIONS] CONTAINER
```

An example is given below:

$ docker export my_space > file.tar

Or

$ docker export --output="file.tar" my_space

With this command, the contents of the containers which are associated with the containers will not be exported. What about a volume which has been mounted on top of a directory existence in a container? In this case, the contents of the underlying directory will be exported, but not the contents of the volume.

The "history" command

This command shows the history of what you have been doing. It takes the following syntax:

```
docker history [OPTIONS] IMAGE
```

If you need to see the latest image which was created in our system, just run the following command:

```
$ docker history docker
```

This will show you all the images which have been created on your system.

If you need to know the process used to add the apache image to your base image, just run the following command:

```
$ docker history docker:scm
```

Just run the command on your system, and then observe what will happen.

Images

By default, this command will give you all of the high level images in your system, their tags, repositories, and virtual size. The command takes the following syntax:

```
docker images [OPTIONS] [REPOSITORY]
```

The intermediate layers which are contained in images and which are responsible for increasing usability, decreasing the disk usage, and increasing the speed of building the Docker will not be shown by this command. The virtual size is the cumulative size which the image and its parent images take. If the image has more than one tag and repository names, then it will be listed more than once.

To list the images which have been created recently, use the following command:

```
$ docker images
```

You will get the details of each of the images. These include the tag, the ID, the name, the size, and other details associated with the images.

```
TAG
<none>
latest
<none>
latest
<none>
```

To list the image IDs in full length, just use the following command:

```
$ docker images --no-trunc
```

The command will give you the full length of your Image IDs. An example of an image ID I get from the above command is given below:

```
78a85c484f71509adeaace20e72e941f6bdd2b25b4c75da8693efd9f61a37921
```

Image Digests

The digest is the content-addressable identifier found in images which use the V2 or just a later format. If you do not change the input which you are using to generate the image, then the digest will be predictable. For to see the digest values for our images, we use the flag "—*digests*" together with the command. This is shown below:

```
$ docker images --digests
```

Just run the command, and then observe the digest value that you get. In my case, I get the following:

```
sha256:abbf3f9a99c48fc460d422912b6a5adgg7dfbb951d8fb2e4a98cab0382cfadbg
```

During the pull or push of an image to the 2.0 Registry, the digest value will always be shown. While pulling an image from the Registry such as the Docker Hub, you can choose to use the digest.

Filtering

For this purpose, we use the filtering flag, which is "*-f*" or "*-filter.*" You can pass more flags in case there are numerous filters.

Consider the command given below:

```
$ docker images --filter "dangling=true"
```

What happens with the command is that it will display all the images in the system which are not tagged, that is, the leaves of image tree, but not the intermediaries.

These are the kind of images which result once the "*repo:tag*" is taken away from the image ID during a new build of an image, meaning that it will be left untagged. In case you try to remove an image which is currently being used by the container, then you will get or receive a warning about the same. Another example is given below:

```
$ docker rmi $(docker images -f "dangling=true" -q)
```

The command will display all of the images which are ready to be used by the "docker rmi ..." In case there are containers which are using the images which are not tagged, and then you will also be warned.

Chapter 2- Management of Complex Docker Containers

Docker containers are highly used in production environments. Due to the nature of this environment, the containers used in this case are very complex. One needs to know how to manage these. This will be explored in this chapter.

The Docker Machine Beta

This tool was recently introduced, and it can help you to move from nothing to a very complex Docker container. It can be used for creation of Docker containers on your machine, in cloud environments, in data centers, and then it is used for configuration of the Docker client so as to communicate to these. It is used as follows:

```
$ docker-machine create -d virtualbox dev
```

On execution of the above command, everything will be set up. This will download the Machine and then install it on your computer. Notice the use of the "-d" flag, which will run the process in the background. The command will run in a verbose manner, and you will observe the following output as it runs:

```
[info] Downloading boot2docker...
[info] Creating SSH key...
[info] Creating VirtualBox VM...
[info] Starting VirtualBox VM...
[info] Waiting for VM to start...
[info] "dev" has been created and is now the active machine.
[info] To point your Docker client at it, run this in your shell: $(docker-
machine env dev)
```

This shows that it tells or informs you of how it is progressing. Once the above command completes its execution, just run the following command:

```
$ $(docker-machine env dev)
```

There will be no observed output from the above command. Next, just run the following command so as to test whether or not the installation ran successfully:

```
$ docker run busybox echo hello world
```

What the above command does is that it checks for the presence of the *"busybox"* image in your local system. If it is not available, it will download it from the Docker Hub. The image will then be executed, and you will observe some text on the output. The command will run in a verbose manner, and in my case, I get the following output:

```
Unable to find image 'busybox' locally
Pulling repository busybox
e72ac664f4f0: Download complete
511136ea3c5a: Download complete
df7546f9f060: Download complete
e433a6c5b276: Download complete
hello world
```

As shown in the above figure, the command has finally printed the "*hello world*" message. The image was not found locally, so this is why it has been pulled from the Docker Hub.

How to run a Dockerized App

Installation of the Docker is very easy. Once you have installed it, you need to run the dockerized application. With the Docker, a Registry which contains public applications is maintained which are made available as public images. In this section, we will explore how to use the "JSDetox" JavaScript deobfuscation tool in your Docker.

There are a number of packages which need to be installed alongside this package. The problem is that most of these packages might end up conflicting with the ones you have already installed. However, due to the distribution property provided by the Docker, this problem is solved.

The image for this can be run by executing the following command:

```
sudo docker run --rm -p 3000:3000 remnux/jsdetox
```

Once the above command has been executed, open your browser, and then enter the following URL:

http://localhost:3000

In my system, I get the following output from the previous command:

```
Unable to find image 'remnux/jsdetox' locally
Pulling repository remnux/jsdetox
e67922e7631f: Pulling dependent layers
511136ea3c5a: Download complete
5bc37dc2dfba: Download complete
61cb619d86bc: Download complete
3f45ca85fedc: Download complete
78e82ee876a2: Download complete
dc07507cef42: Download complete
86ce37374f40: Download complete
1090a4caef8f: Download complete
23346e488b6d: Download complete
59df903857f3: Downloading [======>
```

In case you are using either Mac OS X or the Windows operating system, the steps can be a bit tricky. However, with the assistance of the boot2docker tool, this will become easy. You just have to connect the IP address of the virtual machine being set up by the Docker. As shown in the above figure, the image which we have specified, that is *"remnux/jsdetox,"* was not found in the local system, so it was downloaded from the Docker Registry. After running the JSDetox, it will begin to listen from the port number 3000. However, we will be unable to access the port from our container, due to the fact that it is running from a container. We have to redirect to the port so that we get the following output:

The above will be the output on the browser once we execute the URL which we previously gave.

Building process

Suppose that we want to build the Docker image for the application. To do this, we can start with the core image of the core OS, and then run it in the Docker. Necessary tools can then be installed, and then perform the necessary configurations. Consider the command given below:

```
FROM ubuntu:14.04
```

What the command does is that it will instruct the Docker to use the Ubuntu's 14.04 public license as the base image of the image we are going to create. Consider the next instructions given below:

```
USER root

RUN apt-get update && apt-get install -y git ruby ruby-dev ...
```

What the commands do is that they will instruct for the OS to be upgraded, and for some packages to be installed. These are the packages which the JSDetox needs so as to be able to run. Note that the command *"apt-get"* should be run while having the administrative privileges. Consider the next command given below:

```
RUN groupadd -r nonroot -g 433 && useradd -u 431 -r -g nonroot ...
```

What the above command does is that it adds a group and a user named *"nonroot"* to our image. This means that we will be able to run or launch the JSDetox without having the administrative privileges. Consider the next commands given below:

```
USER nonroot

WORKDIR /home/nonroot

RUN git clone https://github.com/svent/jsdetox.git

RUN apt-get update && apt-get install -y git ruby ruby-dev ...
```

The commands shown above are responsible for the downloading of the JSDetox from the GitHub repository. This will be done as a *"nonroot"* user.

The next commands are given below:

```
WORKDIR /home/nonroot/jsdetox

RUN bundle install
```

What they do is that they will install the JSDetox into the system.

Now that we have accomplished the task of downloading and installation, we need to establish a way how it will be launched or started. Consider the commands given below:

```
WORKDIR /home/nonroot/jsdetox

CMD ./jsdetox -l $HOSTNAME 2>/dev/null
```

When the above commands are executed, you will have specified how the JSDetox application will be started by the Docker once the container is launched. You will then be done.

Chapter 3- Docker Deployment tools

Docker deployment can frustrate most of the Docker users. However, there are tools which have been developed so as to help in solving this problem. Let us discuss some of these tools.

Captainhook

We need to demonstrate how we can use this tool so as to deploy the Docker. In the configuration directory, you should have a configuration file with the following code:

```
{
"scripts": [
{
"command": "/root/gablog.sh",
"args": [
"4"
]
}
]
}
```

Note that in the above code, we have a script named *"gablosh.sh."* The following is the code for the script:

/root/gablog.sh

```
if [ -z "$1" ]
then
echo "usage : gablog.sh 4 -- starting four new instances"
exit -1
fi
echo "Getting the gablog containers which are currently running"
OLDPORTS=( `docker ps | grep gacademy-web | awk '{print $1}'` )
echo "pull the new version"
docker pull bkn/gacademy-web
echo "Launching new containers"
for j in `seq 1 $1` ; do
docker          run          -d          -e
VIRTUAL_HOST=blog.gacademy.com     -p     80
bkn/gacademy-web
done
echo "remove the old containers"
for j in ${OLDPORTS[@]}
do
```

echo "remove the old container $j"

docker kill $j

done

The container might look complicated to some of you. However, it looks for the containers which are running, and then it stores them. For the case of the old containers, they are deleted from the system. You can then run the command given below:

```
$> captainhook -listen-addr=0.0.0.0:8080 -echo -configdir /root/captainhook &
```

The command will launch captainhook and the configuration directory which we have specified. You can then use curl for the purpose of testing this:

```
$> curl http://127.0.0.1:8080/gablog.json
```

A simple response from the server should be observed. The container should also be running by this time, and this can be verified by execution of the *"docker ps"* command. To make the script *"gablog.sh"* executable, use the following command:

chmod +x gablog.sh

The deployment process will give us the following:

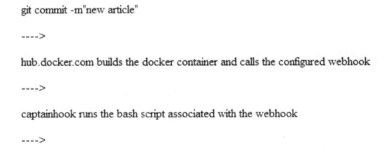

git commit -m"new article"

---->

hub.docker.com builds the docker container and calls the configured webhook

---->

captainhook runs the bash script associated with the webhook

---->

Chapter 4- Networking in the Docker

Networking is very important and essential for Docker containers. This is because it is highly used in servers, ISPs, and in data centers. Let us learn some of the commands which can be used for the purpose of networking in the Docker.

You might need to find the interface of the Docker. By default, the Docker has an interface named *"docker0"* which can be used for connection to the outside world. By default, the IP address "172.17.42.1/16" will be assigned to this interface, and this will act as the subnet of all the IP address which are running.

Consider the command given below:

```
# ip a
```

```
# ip a
```
After executing the above command in my system, I get the following as the output:

```
root@linux:~# ip a
1: lo: <LOOPBACK,UP,LOWER_UP> mtu 65536 qdisc noqueue state UNKNOWN group default
    link/loopback 00:00:00:00:00:00 brd 00:00:00:00:00:00
    inet 127.0.0.1/8 scope host lo
       valid_lft forever preferred_lft forever
    inet6 ::1/128 scope host
       valid_lft forever preferred_lft forever
2: eth0: <BROADCAST,MULTICAST,UP,LOWER_UP> mtu 1500 qdisc pfifo_fast state UP group default q
en 1000
    link/ether 04:01:4f:2a:9a:01 brd ff:ff:ff:ff:ff:ff
    inet 45.55.231.27/18 brd 45.55.255.255 scope global eth0
       valid_lft forever preferred_lft forever
    inet6 fe80::601:4fff:fe2a:9a01/64 scope link
       valid_lft forever preferred_lft forever
3: docker0: <NO-CARRIER,BROADCAST,MULTICAST,UP> mtu 1500 qdisc noqueue state DOWN group defau
t
    link/ether 56:84:7a:fe:97:99 brd ff:ff:ff:ff:ff:ff
    inet 172.17.42.1/16 scope global docker0
       valid_lft forever preferred_lft forever
```

The command is used to tell us more about the bridge interface for *"docker0"* and know the containers which are connected to it. The command should be run inside the terminal or inside the shell where the Docker has been installed.

It is also good for one to know the IP address of their Docker container. We should begin by starting a new container, which can be done by use of a command similar to the one given below:

docker run -it ubuntu

In case you already have a running container, you skip running the above command. So as to get the IP address of the container which is currently running, we can use the command *"ip a"* as shown below:

This command will give you all of the details necessary to be known about the bridge interface:

```
1: lo: <LOOPBACK,UP,LOWER_UP> mtu 1500 qdisc noqueue state UNKNOWN group default
    link/loopback 00:00:00:00:00:00 brd 00:00:00:00:00:00
    inet 127.0.0.1/8 scope host lo
       valid_lft forever preferred_lft forever
    inet6 ::1/128 scope host
       valid_lft forever preferred_lft forever
8: eth0: <BROADCAST,UP,LOWER_UP> mtu 1500 qdisc pfifo_fast state UP group default qlen 10
    link/ether c2:32:1c:63:6b:c0 brd ff:ff:ff:ff:ff:ff
    inet 172.17.0.4/16 scope global eth0
       valid_lft forever preferred_lft forever
    inet6 fe80::c032:1cff:fe63:6bc0/64 scope link
       valid_lft forever preferred_lft forever
```

It is good for us to expose the port which has been configured in the Dockerfile of our container to the high port. In this case, we use the "*-P*" flag. The random port of the Docker container will then be opened to the port which is defined by the Dockerfile. An example is given in the following example:

```
# docker run -itd -P httpd
```

The port of the container will be mapped to port number 80, as the Dockerfile of the httpd defines this. To know whether this has happened, you just have to view the container which is running by the following command:

```
# docker ps
```

The above command will show us the exposed port. The curl command can be used for the purpose of checking this as shown below:

```
# curl http://localhost:49153
```

If it is working effectively on your system, you will be informed of this as shown below:

```
<html><body><h1>It works!</h1></body></html>
```

The output shows that the configuration was successful.

We might also need to perform the mapping in a specific manner in which we will map to a specific port. In this case, the port should be defined by use of the "-p" flag. This is shown in the command given below:

```
# docker run -itd -p 8080:80 httpd
```

With the above command, the port number 8080 will be mapped to the port number 80. To check whether we have succeeded, we can run the curl command as shown below:

```
# curl http://localhost:8080
```

If you get a message that it works, then you are set.

For our containers to be assigned a custom IP address, a new bridge interface needs to be created. We will create one and give it the name *"bridgeo."* We will then assign it an IP address. Consider the following sequence of commands:

```
# stop docker.io

# ip link add bridge0 type bridge

# ip addr add 172.30.2.1/20 dev bridge0

# ip link set bridge0 up

# docker -d -b bridge0
```

Just write and then execute the commands given above. We will have created the Docker Bridge, and also have assigned an IP address to it. The next step involves informing the Docker daemon about the same. This can be done by use of the following commands:

```
# echo 'DOCKER_OPTS="-b=bridge0"' >> /etc/default/docker

# service docker.io start
```

Once you have executed the above commands, you should get output such as the one given below:

```
docker.io start/running, process 4277
```

It is also possible for us to link one image to another. In this case, we use the "-*flag.*" First, we should use the "-*name*" flag, so as to make it easy for us to denote the image. This is shown below:

docker run -d --name db images/postgres

Once we are done with the above command, we can then link the image "*images/myapp*" and the image "*database.*" The resulting image will be named "*finalimage.*" This is shown below:

docker run -d -P --name finalimage --link database:database images/myapp python app.py

Just type the command correctly and then execute it. It will then run and then complete. You will have joined the two images into a unit image named "*finalimage.*"

Chapter 5- Orchestration in the Docker

We need to orchestrate the Docker, and especially when using it in production environments. The Docker community released some tools which can be used for this purpose. Let us discuss some of these tools.

The Docker Swarm

This tool is used for the purpose of hosting and scheduling a cluster of Docker containers. You will learn about how to create a Docker Swarm on your machine and VirtualBox.

Each of the nodes used in the Docker Swarm should be in a position to access the Docker Hub for downloading and running images in your container. To create a Docker Swarm on your machine, follow the steps given below:

1. List all the machines available in your system. Use the following command:

```
$ docker-machine ls
```

2. Create a VirtualBox machine and give it the name *"local."* Use the command given below:

```
$ docker-machine create -d virtualbox local
```

3. The machine which has been created should then be loaded into the shell. Use the following command:

```
$ eval "$(docker-machine env local)"
```

4. You should then use the Docker Swarm image so as to generate a discovery token. The following command can be used for this purpose:

```
$ docker run swarm create
```

If the latest image of *"swarm:latest"* is not found in your local system, it will be pulled to your system. The command will run verbosely, and you will observe the following output:

```
latest: Pulling from swarm
de939d6ed512: Pull complete
79195899a8a4: Pull complete
79ad4f2cc8e0: Pull complete
0db1696be81b: Pull complete
ae3b6728155e: Pull complete
57ec2f5f3e06: Pull complete
73504b2882a3: Already exists
swarm:latest: The image you are pulling has been
Digest: sha256:aaaf6c18b8be01a75099cc554b4fb372b
Status: Downloaded newer image for swarm:latest
```

5. The token should then be saved in a safe place.

Launching the Swarm Manager

This is the one responsible for orchestrating and scheduling containers in the entire system. The process of hosting the containers is done by the Swarm agents. They are a kind of regular Docker daemon which you can communicate with via the Docker remote API. Let us try to create two Swarm managers:

1.   Under your VirtualBox, create a Swarm manager. This is shown below:

```
$ docker-machine create -d virtualbox --swarm --swarm-master --swarm-discovery token://ae0cd96a72cf06dba8c1c4aa79536fc3 swarm-master
```

2.   Open the VirtualBox Manager, which should have the "_local_" machine and the "_swarm-master_" machine which we have just created. These are shown below:

3.

4.   Create the swarm node:

```
$ docker-machine create -d virtualbox --swarm --swarm-discovery token://ae0cd96a72cf06dba8c1c4aa79536fc3 swarm-agent-00
```

5.   Create another agent, and give it the name "*swarm-agent-1*". This is shown below:

```
$ docker-machine create -d virtualbox --swarm --swarm-discovery token://ae0cd96a72cf06dba8c1c4aa79536fc3 swarm-agent-1
```

The two agents should now be available in your VirtualBox.

Directing the Swarm

What we need to do is to establish a connection to the swarm, show the information related to it, and then start the image related to the swarm. Follow the steps given below:

1. Begin by running the following command:

    ```
    $ eval $(docker-machine env --swarm swarm-master)
    ```

    The Docker environment will be pointed to the machine which is running the swarm master.

2. Use the *"docker"* command so as to get information about your new swarm:

    ```
    $ docker info
    ```

Note that at this moment, the master is running both the swarm agent container and the swarm manager. However, this is not a good technique in a production environment since the agent can develop problems.

Chapter 6- Security in the Docker

The security of the Docker is very important. This is because it is used in production environments. If its security is not enhanced, then private data and information can be lost and get into wrong hands.

The first measure of ensuring security in the Docker is the use of the "*docker*" group.. If you do not how to do this, consult the book "Docker. The first look" by Kevin Watts. Users who have been added to this group can freely access the computer and carry out any tasks including modifying the file systems. This explains why you need to be careful while adding users to the group. Only the trusted users should be added to the group.

Also, the Docker has also introduced the flag "*--security-opt*" to the command line. With this flag, the users will be able to set AppArmor and SELinux profiles and labels. Suppose that you came up with a policy which allows the container to listen only to Apache ports. If this policy was defined in svirt_apache, then it can be applied to your container by use of the following command:

```
$ docker run --security-opt label:type:svirt_apache -i -t ubuntu \ bash
```

This will make the process of running docker-in-docker by the users very easy as they will not have to use the *"docker run – privileged"* on the above kernels.

Conclusion

It can be concluded that the Docker is a very important and very useful project. The Docker can be used to perform more complex tasks, and especially in production environments. When used in production environments, the Docker is normally installed in the Linux operating system.

However, this is not a must since some organizations also use other types of operating systems in their production environments. This explains why you need to clearly understand how the Docker can be installed in the various distributions of Linux. This was explored in the "Docker. The first look" by Kevin Watts, so if you do not know how to perform it, just goes through the book.

The security of the Docker in these environments is very key. This is why you need to understand the various security measures which can be taken to secure the Docker. These have been discussed in this book. Networking in the Docker is also very crucial. For instance, it is possible for one to join two Docker images into a single image, and this has been explored in this book. There are also important networking commands for the Docker which has been discussed in this book.

The Docker command line is also very powerful, and can be used to run complex commands. Most of these commands have been discussed in this book. To deploy the Docker into a working environment, one can use tools. You need to understand some of these tools so that you can make use of them. My hope is that you are now in a position to carry out complex tasks with the Docker.

www.ingramcontent.com/pod-product-compliance
Lightning Source LLC
Chambersburg PA
CBHW071030050326
40689CB00014B/3587